GOD CARES WHEN SOMEBODY HURTS ME

BY ELSPETH CAMPBELL MURPHY
ILLUSTRATED BY JANE E. NELSON

Chariot Books

GOD CARES WHEN SOMEBODY HURTS ME

BY ELSPETH CAMPBELL MURPHY
ILLUSTRATED BY JANE E. NELSON

Chariot Books is an imprint of David C. Cook Publishing Co.
David C. Cook Publishing Co., Elgin, Illinois 60120
David C. Cook Publishing Co., Weston, Ontario

GOD CARES WHEN SOMEBODY HURTS ME

Verses taken from the *Holy Bible: New International* Version © 1978 by the New York International Bible Society. Used by permission of Zondervan.
First printing, 1984
Printed in the United States of America
89 88 87 86 85 84 5 4 3 2 1

Library of Congress Cataloging in Publication Data

Murphy, Elspeth Campbell.
God cares when somebody hurts me.
[1. Friendship—Fiction. 2. Christian life—Fiction]
I. Nelson, Jane E., ill. II. Title.
PZ7.M95316Gr 1984   [E]   83-72502
ISBN 0-89191-790-X

This afternoon my friend and I
were walking over to my house, God.
It was raining, and we were going to stay inside
and play Parcheesi and make popcorn.

But then some older girls came along.
They said they were going to play games at their house.
"Come with us," they said to my friend.
"You don't want to go to *her* house," they said,
and they pointed at me.

You know what my friend did, God?
She went with those other girls!
"OK," I yelled at her.
"Just *be* that way!
See if *I* care!
But I won't be your friend anymore."

If she wants to be my friend again
that's too bad for her.
She hurt me, God.

I wouldn't be her friend even if she came
over and made my bed every day for a week.
I wouldn't be her friend even if she
let me ride her ten-speed bike.

My friend really *hurt* me, God!
So what if she didn't scratch me
or push me down?
She still hurt me—
she hurt my *feelings.*
And now my chest feels like there's
a big, heavy rock sitting on it.

But do you know what, God?
It's lonely when you have to eat popcorn
all by yourself.
And it's boring to watch tv
all alone.

11

My friend *should* have come to my house.
And those girls *should* have invited me to go with them, too.

13

I know you understand
how I feel about that, God.
I think it probably hurts you
when people don't pay attention to you or your rules.
I think maybe I've hurt you sometimes.

14

But that doesn't mean you stop caring about me—
or tell me you won't be my friend anymore.
That's not the way you act.
And no matter how hard it is,
you want me to copy you
and act right.

Guess what, God?
My friend just came by my house.
She's standing in my yard.

"What're you doing?" she asks me. And she talks so quietly I almost can't hear her.

"Nothing," I say. "Anyway, I thought you were playing with those other kids."

"Oh, they're just dumb," she says, not looking at me. Then she says, "I'll play with you. . . ."
And the way she says it, God, it's like she's asking me if I'll still be her friend.

18

She shouldn't have gone off and left me, God,
but I think I understand why she did.
Those older kids just made her feel
grown up and important.
For a while, anyway.

I tell my friend,
"If you want, you can play with me."
And I think maybe you're smiling, God.
Know why?

22

Because I'm trying to act
the way you tell me to in your Word:

Be kind and compassionate
to one another,
forgiving each other,
just as in Christ
God forgave you.

Ephesians 4:32*

This verse is found on page———in
my Bible.

23

*This verse is taken from the New International Version
of the Bible, but you may use the version of your choice.

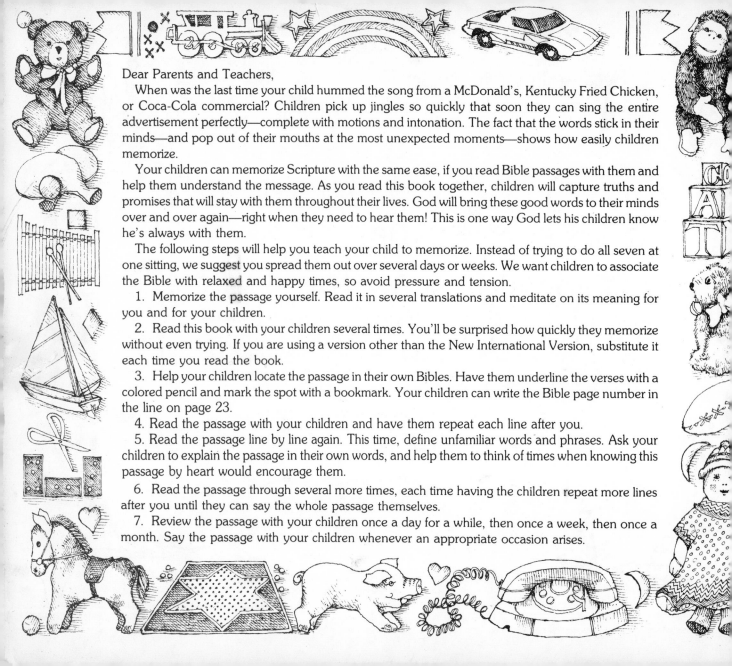

Dear Parents and Teachers,

When was the last time your child hummed the song from a McDonald's, Kentucky Fried Chicken, or Coca-Cola commercial? Children pick up jingles so quickly that soon they can sing the entire advertisement perfectly—complete with motions and intonation. The fact that the words stick in their minds—and pop out of their mouths at the most unexpected moments—shows how easily children memorize.

Your children can memorize Scripture with the same ease, if you read Bible passages with them and help them understand the message. As you read this book together, children will capture truths and promises that will stay with them throughout their lives. God will bring these good words to their minds over and over again—right when they need to hear them! This is one way God lets his children know he's always with them.

The following steps will help you teach your child to memorize. Instead of trying to do all seven at one sitting, we suggest you spread them out over several days or weeks. We want children to associate the Bible with relaxed and happy times, so avoid pressure and tension.

1. Memorize the passage yourself. Read it in several translations and meditate on its meaning for you and for your children.

2. Read this book with your children several times. You'll be surprised how quickly they memorize without even trying. If you are using a version other than the New International Version, substitute it each time you read the book.

3. Help your children locate the passage in their own Bibles. Have them underline the verses with a colored pencil and mark the spot with a bookmark. Your children can write the Bible page number in the line on page 23.

4. Read the passage with your children and have them repeat each line after you.

5. Read the passage line by line again. This time, define unfamiliar words and phrases. Ask your children to explain the passage in their own words, and help them to think of times when knowing this passage by heart would encourage them.

6. Read the passage through several more times, each time having the children repeat more lines after you until they can say the whole passage themselves.

7. Review the passage with your children once a day for a while, then once a week, then once a month. Say the passage with your children whenever an appropriate occasion arises.